Abraham's Diner

Simple wisdom for more control, focus, and inspiration

DANNY BADER

Dedication

To all of us doing the hard work
to make Life easy...press on!

Contents

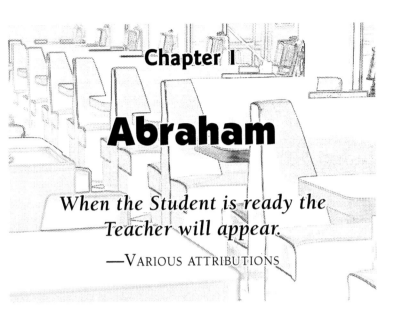

Chapter 1

Abraham

When the Student is ready the
Teacher will appear.

—Various attributions

WE DIDN'T TALK too much that first day when he came in. But after a little while, like most of them, we did. I could tell he's a good man, always has been—seems he just needed to be slowed down a bit.

I'm Abraham. I've had this diner quite a few years on this little corner in this sleepy, beach-side town. Well, I guess it used to be sleepy. Not so much anymore. Businesses moved in and houses went up—big houses. Yep, this old town is now one of the places many people want to live. You should see the spiffy-dressed people who shop along these few blocks and come in to get a bite to eat or a cup of coffee. Some of the cars are real fancy. A lot from overseas.

Kind of crazy to me, all this change, but all good. I bought this diner a long time ago from old Sam Jennings for a handshake and promise to pay him $25,000 over however long it took me. And I did. I remember Sam saying, "Abraham, you paid faster than I thought. You sure you don't need any more time?" Now, there was a really fine man. I miss old Sam. I'm told once or twice a week that my diner and the parking lot that goes with it are probably worth a few million. Well, I guess when I go some-one will get the money. My lawyer and I have an idea in place in case I go before I'm expecting. (Guess most people go before they're expecting to.)

I remember the first time Patrick walked into my diner. It was March, raining like it hadn't rained in a long time, really pissing down, and we needed it. We always do. He jumped out of a fan-cy black car. He didn't have an umbrella so he ran in quickly. His salt-and-pepper hair was dripping wet. He shook off a bit and caught my eye as I flipped a few eggs. "Morning," I called out, smiling. "You're welcome to sit wherever you'd like."

He sat at a small table by the front window. I walked over and extended my hand. He looked a bit surprised as he was drying off the reading glasses that had been up on his head when he came in. He shook my hand then pulled his iPhone from his pocket.

"I'm Abraham," I said.

"Oh, nice to meet you. I'm Patrick," he said distractedly. "Abra-ham?—I guess you own this place?"

"Nope, just got the same name as the guy who does." He looked puzzled until I smiled, giving him a wink. "Coffee, I'm guessing. Black, right?"

"Yes. How'd you know?"

"Not sure. I just do." I walked to the counter and returned with the coffee. "So, Patrick . . . do you know what you'd like?"

He placed the menu back into the wire holder next to the sugar and condiments. "Yes. How about two eggs over medium, bacon—well done—and some rye toast."

I nodded. "I can do that, Patrick. And how about a scoop of home fries? Not too fattening and I use a special seasoning that folks seem to like."

Patrick smiled slightly. "Sounds good." He wasn't looking at me; his focus had shifted to the phone.

Patrick ate that first meal I served him; although, I wasn't sure how he did it without dropping any food in his lap—his eyes were on that phone most of the time. I did see him look out the window a few times—followed by a sigh or deep, silent breath. There were quite a few people, mostly regulars, in our place that morning. Patrick didn't really notice them.

Afterward, he walked out the door to his nice car, in his nice suede loafers, and I thought, *Man, someone ought to suggest to Patrick that he not wear suede loafers in the rain—and maybe get himself an umbrella.*

Gwen came up next to me as I watched Patrick's car pull away. "Know that guy?" she asked. Gwen had been with me for a long while. She smiled her wonderful smile, so full of gleaming white teeth. *And all original after all these years*, she always tells customers. They always laugh.

"Not yet. Just met this morning," I responded with a sideways glance. "Seems like a nice man."

"Oh, I've seen that look before," said Gwen. "You'll know him okay; you'll know him." She walked away chuckling to herself.

* * *

Two weeks later, Patrick came in again for breakfast. The sun was up, the air was fresh, not a cloud in the sky. It was a perfect Saturday. As Patrick walked through the door, I noticed a young man following him. His baseball hat sat backwards on his head, long blond hair hanging down. His eyes were glued to his iPhone. Neither spoke to the other.

Patrick saw me looking at him and gave me a nod. I pointed to a booth along the wall and arrived there a minute later. The boy did not look up. Patrick did. "Hi, Abraham."

"Hi, Patrick. Nice to see you again."

"Luke, can you put your phone down for a minute and say hi to Abraham. He owns this place."

The young man placed his phone on the table and held out his hand. "Hi, Abraham, nice to meet you. I have a few friends that come in here and they say the breakfast is awesome."

"Glad to meet you, Luke. And glad your friends like our food," I replied, not having expected his friendliness. "Is this your first time in?"

"Yeah. I told my dad the other day we should do something together this weekend, so here we are."

I took their order and stopped at another table on the way back to the kitchen. I turned back to look at Patrick, who was back on his phone. Luke was looking at him. He took a deep breath, glanced briefly out the window, and then grabbed his phone as well. I dropped off their food a few minutes later. Aside from a few comments, it looked like they ate their breakfast in silence. Forks in right hands, phones in left.

"You guys have big plans today?" I asked as I cleared their plates. "Maybe some surfing or beach time? Or a round of golf?"

Luke responded, "Man, some surfing would be great, but I think my dad has to work."

Patrick looked up. "Yes, I do have some work to do. It just never seems to let up, and I feel like I'm always behind." He took a deep breath.

"But, Dad, you always used to tell Joey and me you'd do some surfing with us when we moved out here. Joey and I love this one break, and I know you'd have fun too. Remember you told us about all that surfing you did growing up in Cape May and Wildwood?"

"I do, Luke," Patrick said abruptly. "But those times were different. I was like you and Joey. I was young. I can't waste time surfing now. I need to work, to keep up, so we can afford to live here. And you and your brother and Mom can have all the nice things you have. You understand, don't you? Trust me, you'll see some day."

Luke's smile seemed a little forced when he answered. "Yeah, I understand, Dad. And I do appreciate what you do for us. Just seems weird that we live in this great beach town, with great waves, and you never surf anymore. Kind of like a line my teacher told us the other day, he said 'Too many people are standing knee deep in a river and dying of thirst.'"

"Yeah, well, I'm guessing your teacher doesn't get a third of the e-mails and interruptions I get every day." Patrick stood up and shook my hand. "See you again soon."

Luke rose and also shook my hand. "Great to meet you, Abraham. My friends were right, the food here is great." He began following his dad towards the door.

"Glad you enjoyed it," I said. "And, Luke." He turned. "I'll keep an eye out for you in the line-up. I still get out and catch a few waves."

Luke smiled. "Cool."

I watched them walk to the car in silence.

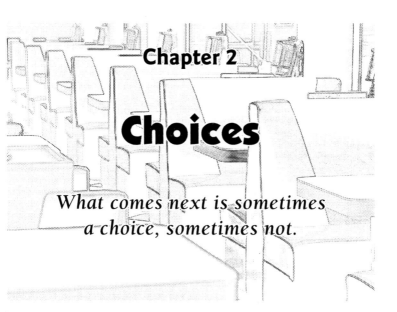

Chapter 2

Choices

*What comes next is sometimes
a choice, sometimes not.*

A WEEK LATER, I was sitting in the diner with my friend Cliff. He's been coming in for years. Cliff is a father of four grown kids and has quite a few grandkids. His good mood was perpetual, but even more so when some of the little ones were coming. He'd been quite successful in the TV business just up the coast, but was pretty much retired now.

Cliff took a sip of coffee. "A neighbor of mine said he was in for the first time a few weeks ago. Sounded to me like he had a nice breakfast and liked your place. He said you took care of him."

"That's nice to hear, Cliff. Who was it?—Not that I remember everyone who comes in here."

"His name is Patrick Kendall. Nice guy. He moved in about a year ago with his wife, Lori, and two teenage sons."

I smiled slightly; well, I guess it was more of a grin.

"O-kay," Cliff drawled out. "I've seen that look before. Do you remember Patrick?"

I nodded. "Yes, I believe I do. Nice black BMW? Suede shoes? Full head of hair, on the long side, a splash of gray?"

"That would be him."

"He's actually been in twice. The last time, a few weekends ago, he had his son Luke with him. What's he into?"

Cliff shifted in his seat, took his glasses off, and rubbed his eyes. "He's been in the consulting world for some time. He was initially a partner in a nice-sized CPA firm back on the East Coast—Philadelphia, I think—then he moved out here to work for a large firm in their LA office. I get the impression he's pretty bright and moved up the ladder quickly."

Cliff was not looking at me; although, my eyes were on him when he said, "Abraham, I'm not certain," he paused, "he may need you."

* * *

Patrick came back in the following Friday for lunch. He looked like a million bucks in his suit and tie. But something was different about him. He took a seat at the end of the counter, quickly scanned the menu, then traded it in for his phone.

"Hi, Patrick."

"Oh, hi, Abraham."

Patrick ordered and ate his lunch, fingers flying over his phone the whole time. When he was done eating, I placed his check in front of him and asked, "So what you got in store for the rest of today and this weekend, Patrick? Maybe some beach time with the family? Or a round of golf with some friends?"

Patrick sighed as he pulled out his wallet. "I wish. Either one would be great, but I have to work the rest of today, and most of the weekend. I've got a lot of things I need to get done by May and June."

"I'll bet. Like what? Mind me asking?" Patrick looked taken aback.

I continued, "It's okay if you do . . . mind, I mean. I don't want to pry. I've made it my job to connect with as many people as I can and talk with them about all kinds of subjects. Life, death, marriage, divorce, jobs, faith, relationships, fun, healing, travel. You name it, I'll talk about it. I like to get to know them . . . my regulars—and since you've been here now twice before, you qualify as a regular. Ha!"

Patrick's smile came easy and slowly. "Sounds good. It seems I'm only a regular at the office, the airport, and hotels I frequent. I like the thought of being a regular here."

"Well, we're glad to have ya. Guess you're not liking the thought of having to work the next few days?"

"Not really, but I've gotten used to it over the years. I enjoy my work, but the pressure is huge. It seems there's always much more to do than I have time for, and I have so much stuff all over, papers and notes and. . . ." Patrick paused and held up his phone to face me. "And these e-mails are out of control. And, on top of all that, I had two difficult conversations this week—one with my boss and the other with my largest client, Smith, Inc."

He took a deep breath. "And I know I have to have one with my wife, Lori—that will not be fun."

With that, he stood and put some bills on top of the check. "Thanks, Abraham. Keep the change," he said as he pushed it across the counter.

"By the way, it was nice to meet your son Luke. Nice young man."

"Yes, he is. I'm real proud of both my boys. They've been talking about surfing since you brought the subject up with Luke. But I'm just too busy at work. I guess I wish . . . well, to begin with . . . I wish I could just get rid of all this stuff. I just can't find the time for surfing."

"Well, then stop looking for it," I offered, placing the money and check in my apron. Patrick looked puzzled. "Time," I said. "Stop looking for it; it ain't lost." He looked more puzzled. "Patrick, follow me."

"Not sure what you have in mind, Abraham, but I've gotta run. I have a lot of work this afternoon."

"I promise this won't take long," I replied. "Trust me." He nodded slightly and we walked through the kitchen and out onto the small loading dock in the rear of the building. I stood in the sun, relaxed, and breathed deeply and slowly, Patrick next to me.

Patrick glanced at his watch. He spoke first—as they all do. "What are we doing here?"

I waved my hand toward the boxes and cases of drinks stacked at the edge of the platform. Patrick had a blank look on his face.

"I just wanted to show you my stuff. We all have it. Mine is all the supplies that show up here on this loading dock almost daily. For many like you, it's e-mails and notes from meetings and conference calls. Sometimes it's all the requests from others that distract people; sometimes it's all the stuff our kids bring to us from their lives. The point is I just want you to know we all have our stuff. That's all."

I ushered him back into the diner. "Well, it's been good to see you again, Patrick. I wish you the best with your work today. Let me ask you one last question as I walk you out. Do you cook?"

Patrick looked confused. "Not really. My wife does most of the cooking."

As we approached the front door, I continued, "But you can cook an egg, pancakes? And make some toast?"

Patrick grinned. "Yes, I can handle that."

"Good, so how about you come in next Saturday, a week from tomorrow, at 6:00 a.m. and help me cook a bit . . . if you'd like."

Patrick's grin disappeared. "Cook? With you? What the—? Why would I—? I don't have the time—"

I held up my hand for him to stop. "I said if you'd like. I think you'd enjoy the experience. It would be very different from all the stuff you're dealing with—now, get out of here and have a wonderful weekend."

We shook hands and Patrick turned to leave. "And, Patrick." He turned back. "I like your suede loafers and the ones you're wearing now very much, but if you do come next Saturday . . . leave them at home." He turned back to leave but paused to look at the sign above the diner's front door: ***All people here create happiness . . . some by coming and some by going.***

* * *

A few minutes later my friend Emily stopped in. I could tell she'd been out on her run.

"Well, now, don't you look wonderful? And so happy," I said. "How's everything?"

We hugged and Emily held onto my hands. "Feeling so good, Abraham, and happier than I've been in a long time. I've lost twenty pounds—still have more to go—but really have some momentum and moving in the right direction. Work is great; I've finally got my team in place." She emphasized *my*.

"And the rest of that vision?" I inquired.

"Not all great by some standards. Still have some things to work out with Seth, but I'm focused on it." She took a deep breath and let it out. "I'm focused on it."

"Good to hear. You get back on your run, but one thing . . . I may want you to have a talk with a new friend of mine. Maybe we can have breakfast or coffee sometime soon."

She leaned in and kissed my cheek, and turned for the door. "Sure, just let me know."

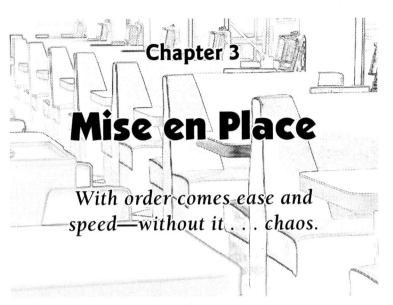

Chapter 3

Mise en Place

With order comes ease and speed—without it . . . chaos.

THE FOLLOWING SATURDAY at 5:50 a.m. I was pleased to see Patrick come in the kitchen door from the loading dock. Not surprised, really—despite Patrick's protestations of too little time.

He walked over to me wearing a serious look, and then smiled as he pulled up one pant leg of his khakis to reveal an old sneaker. "I believe I'm ready."

"I must say you look it." I had just finished laying towels over all the areas on the cooking line except the toaster, large flat grill, and the stove with six burners and frying pans. "Now, here's how this is going to work. We're a team. We open at 6:30 and will get a few folks in then. By about eight o'clock, we'll be full."

Patrick nodded. "Okay, sounds good. What do you want me to do?"

"Gwen, Johnny, and Mary will be working the tables. They'll come back here and give us their orders, and you and I will make the food."

"You sure you wouldn't rather have me taking orders out front? Not sure I'll be very good in the kitchen," Patrick said.

"You'll be fine. There's a menu taped at your spot with the ingredients, in case you don't know how to make something . . . or you can just ask me. Now, go introduce yourself to the others and ask if they need help getting the tables and counter ready. See you back here in about a half hour."

At 6:20, our first customers arrived, and Mary passed along the order: two eggs over easy, bacon, home fries, and wheat toast, and an order of banana pancakes.

"Okay, let's go," I said to Patrick.

He repeated back the order with enthusiasm and began looking around. "Where are the eggs?"

I motioned for him to follow. We went out the door to the loading dock, moved a few boxes, and located a carton of eggs. "Go ahead and grab two, and head back in to get them going," I said. "I've got some things to do back here." He smiled, grabbed the eggs, and rushed back into the kitchen.

About thirty seconds later he was back asking for butter and home fries. Again, we located the items and back to the kitchen he went. This happened again for the pancake mix, bananas, and wheat bread.

It was just about 6:30 when Patrick proudly laid the plates of food—looking okay, I may add—under the heat lamp and rang the bell.

As he was doing that, Gwen and Johnny came in and shouted more orders. Johnny needed two orders of eggs over medium with sausage, one with rye toast and home fries and the other with white toast, no home fries. Gwen needed an order of fruit, a vanilla yogurt, and one Western omelet.

"Okay," I said. "You get the eggs and do the omelet, too. Remember to check the ingredient list by your workstation. I'll prep the banana pancakes, yogurt, and fruit." Patrick followed me to the loading dock. We'd had to move all the cartons around to get the supplies for the first order and they lay scattered around the dock, their contents peaking through open lids: eggs, dairy, fruit, home fries, sausage, yogurt, bread, and rolls. We each grabbed some supplies and got back to the kitchen.

A few minutes later, both Gwen and Johnny popped their heads in and asked about their orders. Patrick didn't reply. He just kept making trips back to the loading dock, slicing vegetables, shredding cheese, and pausing frequently to try to remember what he was supposed to be doing. At about 6:45, he not-so-proudly placed the omelet and egg orders under the heat lamp. I added the toast and fries and rang the bell.

Gwen picked up the omelet order. Johnny paused as he reached for the over-easy eggs. "We need sausage on both of these, not just one," he said.

"Damn. That's my fault, Johnny," said Patrick. "I'm sorry. I'll get it right out. Can you take them to the table, and I'll get the extra sausage as fast as I can."

"No. I don't work like that. I'll wait for the sausage."

Patrick got the sausage out and looked over at me, irritated and shaking his head.

I smiled. "Come on, let's go out back."

"What?" he squeaked, though he followed me towards the dock. "What about the customers? Johnny is already mad at me as it is. I have to finish this order. Once I get used to where everything is, I'm sure I can get faster."

"Patrick," I said, putting my arm around him, "it's okay. Johnny and Gwen can finish up with the current customers and there won't be any others for another quarter hour."

"But I don't understand."

We stood on the loading dock, looking down at the mess. "Patrick, remember what this is?" He shook his head. "This is my stuff, right? We talked about it last week."

"Yes, I remember."

"Here's what to consider. When my stuff arrives on this loading dock, I really shouldn't leave it here. If I do, the food will go bad, and I need it to run my business successfully." He continued shaking his head. "You had to hustle for just four orders already this morning. We'll soon have twice that many to handle at a time, and with chaos like this back here"—I swept my arm across the space—"it's going to be tougher for us to get the orders out, right?"

"You can say that again. It takes a lot of time to pull out all these supplies. I'm trying to move as fast as I can, but I seem to get slower and slower the more things I have to find. I have the sense it's going to be painful this morning . . . especially for me."

"Okay, just relax. We don't really open until 7:00 a.m. I invited a few friends in for a free breakfast on me early this morning.

They're all okay, trust me. Now, come back into the kitchen. There's something I want to show you."

"Abraham?"

"Yes?"

"This feels very weird right now."

"You're not the first person to say that to me!" I smiled and began pulling off the towels I'd placed over the counters. They had been concealing a number of containers with eggs, sliced onions and tomatoes, and shredded cheese. There was a vat of liquid pancake mix with bananas and fresh fruit. Loaves of bread and sliced bagels sat opened on the shelf below the toaster.

I turned to Patrick and in my best French accent declared, "*Mise en place.*"

He laughed. "Meese and what?"

"*Mise en place,*" I repeated. "It's French for *putting in place*. It's been called the religion of good chefs. They call it 'meeze' . . . meaning 'order.' With order, one can move fast and easy."

I walked him through how to prep several of the most common orders using the supplies found in the containers. "No more trips to the loading dock," I said.

"This is great," he answered. "And . . . what if we have Johnny and Gwen write their orders down and I can put them up here." He pointed to the clips on a shelf below the heat lamp. "I got all messed up trying to remember what I needed to do . . . what I needed to make."

"Hmmmm." I smiled. "Sounds good."

We opened at 7:00, and, using our meeze, Patrick and I handled the rush beautifully. At about 10:30, I asked Johnny to take over in the kitchen and Patrick and I made ourselves some food and grabbed a seat in the corner.

"You did a fine job back there," I said. "Thanks."

"Sure, it was fun . . . after we got our meeze on!" he joked. "But why did you want me to do it?"

"Why do you think?" I asked, sipping some tea.

"I'm not sure. I suspect you wanted to teach me a lesson of some sort."

"Patrick, it's like this. Last week you told me you wanted to get rid of all of the stuff cluttering up your life. Remember?"

He nodded, taking another bite of food.

"What I believe is happening is you're leaving all your stuff on your loading dock, and it's piling up, which makes it harder to find things. The more you try to do, the harder it gets to find what you need. You're simply just not set up to move fast and easy. You saw how hard and inconvenient it was to prepare meals while having to work from the boxes of supplies on the loading dock. If I operated the diner that way, I'd be out of business very quickly."

"You sure would." Patrick glanced away in a moment of reflection. "You know just this week I had two different conference calls and I needed information from some e-mails for them. And you know where I went?" he asked. I tilted my head sideways. "I went to my inbox . . . to my loading dock."

"And?"

"And I wasted a lot of time and became very frustrated. I think in hindsight that frustration came out on the call. I was short with some staff and it really wasn't their fault at all."

"Sure. So the trick is that when you read an e-mail or letter or text that you know has information you'll need later or requires a follow-up action on your part, you need to turn it into a form that makes it easier for you to find and use it." I paused. "It looks like you do a lot of correspondence by e-mail. So for you, meeze would mean moving important e-mails right into your calendar."

Patrick pulled out his smartphone and clicked on a few icons. "Can you do that?" he looked puzzled.

"Sure. I've got a friend that teaches much of this. She calls it *converting*. When stuff lands on your version of a loading dock, you need to get really good at converting it into an action in your calendar. What type of system do you use at work?"

"Microsoft Outlook. Does your friend know that system? Can she teach me?"

"Sure. Outlook is what most of her clients have. She does both one-on-one coaching, as well as workshops for larger groups. I know she'd be happy to work with you."

"That would be great, but I don't know when I'd have the time. I'm pretty busy with a lot of client work. Although, this does have me thinking about other e-mails. I have one that I've seen every day for about a week. I need it for this Thursday when I call a client of mine. I wonder how to handle that one?"

"I'm not sure but I think she'd have you convert it." Patrick was still confused. "That is, turn it into what it is. For me, converting the stuff on my loading dock means turning it into ready-to-go ingredients and mixes that make it easy for me to fill orders. All the food is prepped—vegetables chopped, eggs assembled, bread near the toasters, mixes mixed."

Patrick nodded.

"For you, 'to convert' would mean turning an e-mail into a phone call, a follow-up with that person in a few weeks, a report you have to write . . . whatever it is that is required of you. You know, the action you need to take. So with this particular e-mail, turn it into a to-do item and place a due date of this Thursday so you'll see it at the bottom of your calendar."

Patrick was smiling. "Yes, I see. That way the e-mail is out of my inbox . . . my loading dock . . . and I've got my *meeze* in place. Right now, I just leave all my e-mails in my inbox, flagging the ones that require follow up. But then I end up with a whole bunch of flagged e-mails and have to keep re-opening and re-reading them to find what I need."

"Well, I suspect that just slows you down."

"That's for sure. So I guess I'd better find the time to start creating order! What's your friend's name?"

"Cindy. Leave me your card before you take off today and I'll have her send you an e-mail. What else did you pick up this morning?"

"I sure liked when the servers wrote the order out," he replied. "That way I didn't have to try to remember anything."

"Sure. I could tell that was when you began to relax and have some fun," I said. "I know you've got a lot in your head now you're trying to remember and it's not working." Patrick breathed deeply and nodded. "There's another guy I know that comes in once I while; used to live up north a bit in Ojai. Nice fellow, very well-known author and speaker. He once said, 'Your mind is a great place to have an idea, lousy place to hold onto it.'"

"Hmmm. Never really thought about it that way. Makes sense, I guess." He glanced at his watch. "Oh man, I've got to get running, Abraham. Thanks for this morning, and here's my card. And thanks for offering to connect me with Cindy." He was out the door.

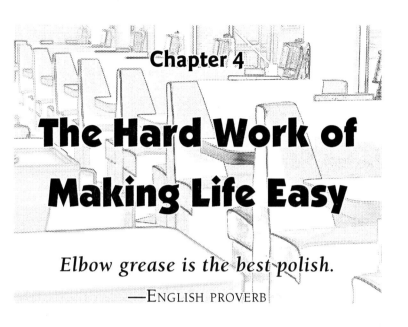

Chapter 4

The Hard Work of Making Life Easy

Elbow grease is the best polish.
—ENGLISH PROVERB

LATER THAT DAY I called Cindy and set up the connection with Patrick. She called about a week later and said they'd met and worked for most of a day.

Cindy was impressed with Patrick's openness to coaching, and his commitment to change. "I have no choice at this point," is what he'd said to her. Cindy agreed to have lunch at the diner and fill me in on the details.

It was another beautiful day late in May. Cindy looked wonderful in jeans, a t-shirt, and sandals. Her t-shirt bore the "jckrbbt" logo used by my friend Brendan.

"Hi, Cindy, it's great to see you as always," I said as we hugged. One of the many things I liked about Cindy is that she held our hugs a little bit longer than the average person, and it felt good.

As we separated, she said, "Nice to see you too, Abraham, it's been too long. You look great. How is life? And the diner?"

"All is good. Getting a few more aches and pains than usual, but age is just a number, right? And how are you? Business good? Anyone special I should know about?"

She laughed. "Business is great; I've got all the business I want at the moment and I'm working with some cool people. The travel has been good, very balanced. And as for someone special," Cindy smiled, "there is this guy I met at my church recently, but too soon to tell." She gave me a wink. "I'll keep you posted."

We sat down. Gwen came and of course Cindy hugged her as well. I'm guessing they could have chatted for an hour had I not playfully cleared my throat.

"So tell me about your work with Patrick," I said. "I mean, I know there's confidentiality with you as his coach, but are you able to give me an overview? He left a message for me with Gwen the day after you two worked together and said he was excited to give it a try, and that it was okay if I talked with you about it."

"Oh, sure. I can fill you in on the high level work and the Outlook piece."

For the next ten minutes, Cindy told me all about the initial day of coaching. She'd gotten to Patrick's office at the agreed-on time, but had to wait for about twenty minutes before Patrick came out to greet her. He'd offered to get Cindy coffee or something else to drink and wondered if she wanted something to eat. "Often, people will go overboard in this small talk if they're uncomfortable or uncertain about our coaching." Cindy chuckled. "Anyhow, we settled into his office and he told me a bit about his role at the firm and about his sons and wife.

"I think I caught him off guard with my first question," she continued. "I asked him how we would know if our sessions were successful. He fumbled for an answer, and then I finally relented and gave him a few nudges by asking about what he wanted to disappear from his life."

This got him going. He told Cindy that his e-mails and over-flowing inbox were a pain in the neck.

"I smiled and glanced at the several piles on his desk and asked, 'What's in these?' to which he replied, 'Good question.' We both laughed a bit."

Cindy had then asked Patrick if they could just take the files to the shredder room. With a slight note of desperation, he'd said, "No. No way."

Cindy pointed out that he didn't even know what was in the piles—so how could he miss what he didn't know he had? "You're right," he'd replied, "but I know that there's something in some of that stuff that I should be paying attention to. And every time I look at the piles I feel stressed."

She'd asked Patrick if he had any "piles in his head," and he got the concept immediately.

"Absolutely," he said. "My head feels very cluttered most of the time." He also told Cindy that he wastes lots of time looking for things, mostly e-mails that are buried in his inbox or sent folder.

"So, then I suggested to him that success for our sessions would be the opposite of what he'd just told me. We'd get him control over his inbox, a clean desk, a head emptied of unknown piles of information, and he'd find it easy to get more done in less time."

Patrick had smiled at this, but was a bit skeptical. "You can do all that?" he'd said.

"And your response?" I inquired as she peered over her mug of green tea.

"Oh, I just said, 'no.'" I smiled at her, shaking my head slightly. Cindy continued, "I told him that I could educate him on *how* this could happen . . . but it was ultimately up to him to *make* it happen. And that I'd support him as much as he wanted. It's like that quote you told me once from Galileo, *You cannot teach a man anything, you can only help him find it within himself.*"

I smiled—that one is a favorite.

Cindy then explained some simple principles about organization and productivity to Patrick. The first was to get a handle on all the stuff that he was thinking about. "We agreed that there were many action items buried in his inbox, in the piles on his desk, and, I suggested, in his head. He agreed with all three."

Cindy then had Patrick write down anything and everything that was in his head. "I told him that if it wasn't something that needed to get done it wouldn't show up," she told me.

Patrick stopped after writing down about a half-dozen items. Cindy urged him to think harder. She asked him, "Anything about the boys or Lori that you might need to do? Anything with

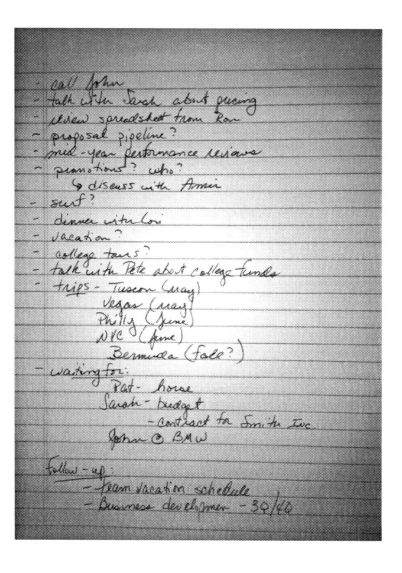

- call John
- talk with Sarah about pricing
- review spreadsheet from Ron
- proposal pipeline?
- mid-year performance reviews
- promotions? who?
  ↳ discuss with Amir
- surf?
- dinner with Lori
- vacation?
- college tours?
- talk with Pete about college funds
- trips - Tuscon (may)
      Vegas (may)
      Philly (june)
      NYC (june)
      Bermuda (fall?)
- waiting for:
      Pat - house
      Sarah - budget
          - contract for Smith Inc.
      John @ BMW

follow-up:
    - team vacation schedule
    - Business development - 30/60

your house or cars?" He added more to the list. "How about any travel or business trips coming up? Anything there?" He wrote more. "What about any calls you need to make, e-mails to send, meetings to schedule?" It was hard to keep up with his scribbling. "Anybody you're waiting for to get back to you? Or you need to follow back up with?"

Cindy had then walked Patrick through the process of converting all these to-dos into tasks in his Outlook program, or to blocks of time on his calendar, depending on the length and priority of the action. "I told him about T, S, A," she said. Patrick asked if she meant the Transportation and Security Administration, but she laughed and told him that it stands for Trash, Save, or Action.

It took a few hours to convert everything written down, then Cindy and Patrick moved on to the piles on his desk. "Patrick told me that a lot of what was in his head was also in his piles," she told me. "He said to me, 'If I get good at converting my paper every day or two, then I probably won't try to remember everything.' I smiled and encouraged him to experiment with that."

"It sounds to me like Patrick is one of the countless people who need to consider a stronger approach to managing all their stuff," I said. "And you were able to shift his thinking, and help him get greater command of Outlook."

"Yes, it was a good morning. As you know, Abraham, the key to people truly evolving lies there—in how they think about what they want to change—about what needs to be different for them—in all the areas of their lives. The afternoon was great as well. He had over three thousand e-mails in his inbox." She'd anchored Patrick to thinking about his e-mails as T, S, A, and he began to get it. Patrick realized he saved too much in files and needed to trash more as well. Cindy had then showed him how to convert e-mails into tasks and calendar appointments.

They'd done a few then Patrick had paused, saying he felt like they were just moving stuff around in Outlook.

"I told him to consider the wisdom of Lincoln," said Cindy. "Lincoln once said, 'Give me six hours to chop down a tree and I will spend the first four sharpening the axe.'"

Patrick had said he agreed with Lincoln, and would probably do the same. Cindy had asked him why, and he'd thought for a few seconds then replied that the work of chopping the tree would go easier and faster. She'd let that thought sit in the silence for moment, then said, "Patrick, it's the same here. When you convert your stuff, you sharpen your axe . . . and your work will get done faster and easier. Will you trust me on this?" He'd nodded.

"By the time I had him review his calendar and the tasks with due dates that showed on the bottom of that calendar view, he finally admitted that my approach might work for him," said Cindy. "I even showed him the Quicksteps function in Outlook that automates the converting of an e-mail. And we set up a few like reply-and-delete and task-and-delete."

By the end of the day, Patrick had converted about fourteen hundred e-mails with Cindy's help, then he'd decided to move the rest to a folder—just as a safety net if he needed to go back to them. "It's not a good use of my time to convert all these old e-mails," he'd commented, "but I'm not ready to trash them just yet. So I'll save them."

Finally, they had downloaded the app on his iPhone and Cindy showed him how his Outlook tasks synched with the app and how he could add actions to the app and they'd sync back to Outlook.

"All in all, it was a great day, and he was very happy," said Cindy. "Patrick kept talking about how much more control he'd be able to get over all his stuff. And that should probably help him relax more and focus on the right things. He has a key client that is due to renew their contract, and while Patrick did not open up completely on this, I sense it may be in jeopardy."

"Smith, Inc. by any chance?" I inquired.

"Yes. You know about it?"

"He mentioned a conversation he'd had with the folks there and I sensed it did not go to well."

Cindy continued, "Good to know, thanks. Patrick kept making comparisons between his morning of cooking with you, and the meeze you two got working, to the work he and I were doing. Of course I agreed with him and offered that I have worked with many bright executives like him, but that their approach to managing their stuff was weak and inconsistent, it had no framework—once they began thinking and behaving differently, they'd report back to me they were saving between six to ten hours per week. He agreed. I then told him that the key for him now was re-wiring how he thought, and of course repetition, repetition, and more repetition. We debriefed the day, scheduled day two of our coaching, and set up a check-in call in between."

Chapter 5

Stillness

Sometimes doing nothing is the best thing to be doing.

I WAS SURPRISED to see Patrick appear at the diner early one Saturday morning a few weeks later. He had his son Luke in tow and another teenage boy I didn't recognize.

"We're here to help," he said. "You remember Luke, my oldest? The other one is Joey. They both said they wanted to do something together this weekend, so I invited them to join me here. When I told them about my cooking with you, they thought it was kind of cool, so I thought it would be a good experience for them to help out around here one morning. They agreed to come—not sure why, I'm guessing Luke told Joey that you surf! So, what do you think, Abraham?"

"Actually, I was hoping we'd do some surfing," mumbled Joey, not exactly looking like a happy camper.

"See," Patrick smiled at me. "Maybe later, Joey." He hugged the boy's shoulder. Then he turned to me. "I've been making some good progress with Cindy and wanted to pay you back for all your help."

"You don't owe me anything, but I'll take all the help I can get," I said. "I want to hear about that progress later on, but right now we've got some meeze to do! C'mon, boys, let's put you to work."

As we walked back into the kitchen, I heard one of the boys whisper to the other, "Did he just say we had to do cheese? What the heck does that mean?"

* * *

Later that morning, Patrick and I grabbed a cup of coffee and sat in a booth while his boys were helping to clean up the kitchen. He filled me in on his work with Cindy, then cleared his throat and asked what must have seemed like an odd question to him.

"Abraham . . . why does Gwen sit in the storeroom with her eyes closed? I saw her back there several times this morning and was worried that something was wrong with her. But I didn't want to pry in case it was something personal."

I smiled. "Oh, it is personal in a way. But there's nothing wrong with Gwen. She's got one of the sharpest minds I know for a lady her age . . . or any lady for that matter. When you see Gwen in there she is just creating some stillness for herself."

Patrick looked confused. "And you're okay with that? I mean, the breakfast shift is short and I just thought maybe you'd want her working, or stocking up, or something. You know, helping with the meeze."

"Oh, I'm quite alright with it. I do it myself a few times a day," I replied. "Stillness has a unique value in our lives."

"With so much to do, I don't really see how stillness can help. I'd rather get as much done as possible so I can clear up time for other things," Patrick said.

"You see, Patrick, when we create stillness and just focus on clearing our head and slowing down our breathing, we actually remove some chemicals from our blood that sometimes don't support us, and the brain replaces them with healthier ones. There's a great deal of research out there on this. When we're working and moving and thinking about our things to do, we often become stressed. Cortisol is a chemical that our brain releases in response to fear or stress. But slowing down and creating some stillness for ourselves engages our vagus nerve, which signals us to slow our breathing, lower our heart rate and blood pressure. Best of all, it lowers our cortisol level. It's like a time-out where we can recover, get more relaxed, and come back to our work with more focus and creativity."

Patrick looked skeptical, but said, "I guess I should know by now to trust your judgment. So, how do you do this stillness thing? Just sit and breathe?"

"Yes, it's that simple. There are many studies suggesting—and even brain scans showing—that a person's brain matter is lost at a greater rate as they age when they don't practice stillness. I saw one study that compared meditators and non-meditators. Quite interesting. The point is that people are healthier when they're older if they practice stillness, and especially if they started when they were younger. In fact, many programs are popping up for children to begin practicing this."

I could see a look of impatience growing on Patrick's face. "But we can talk about the details some other time. . . . Do you ever do this? Just sit still?"

Patrick laughed. "Ha! Me? Never. I'm always trying to do more and go faster."

"Want to try it now? It doesn't take long. Maybe just five minutes."

Patrick stood and looked towards the kitchen. He saw his sons working away, so turned and sat back down. "Yeah . . . I guess. I mean, I don't know if I can do it right."

I offered, "There is no 'right,' Patrick. Just relax; sit straighter. Imagine a string tied to the top of your head pulling it gently toward the ceiling. And close your eyes. We must go 'inside' to reap the most benefit. No talking. Just sit straight and breathe."

Patrick did this for a few minutes. Then he opened his eyes and said, "Wow. This is crazy. I do feel much calmer and relaxed."

"How do you think that would help you back out in the real world?" I asked.

"It feels like my brain has some meeze going on," he said. "Much more order and a lot less noise. I'm guessing this would allow me to get back into my work with greater focus."

"That's been my experience. I suggest you begin to do it more consistently."

"I think I will. No, I definitely will. Thanks, Abraham." He was shaking his head. "You just keep giving me more and more things to think about. Thanks."

"My pleasure, Patrick. Thanks for your help today, and keep some of that relaxed focus around for yourself the rest of the day."

"Well, I'm going to be with my sons, so that may be hard to do. But I'll try." He stood and called to his boys. The three were laughing at something that Joey was saying as they went out the door.

Chapter 6

Progress & Impact

The true value of one's growth
is rarely seen at first glance.

EARLY ONE MORNING, a few days later, I was in the diner clearing a booth when I felt a tap on the shoulder. I turned to see an attractive woman of about forty-five. Her brown hair had some light streaks throughout and her brown eyes seemed to smile.

"Abraham?" she inquired.

I smiled. "Well, even if I wasn't I may claim to be!"

She held out her hand, smiling. "I'm Lori Kendall. I believe you recently gave my husband, Patrick, and my sons, Joey and Luke, a few lessons in diner cooking."

I took her hand, holding it a moment. "Ah, yes. We did have a go at it. Your boys really helped out when they were here, and Patrick is a pretty good cook." I paused. "For a consultant. If that career doesn't work out, I can probably use him around here."

Lori laughed. "I know you're busy, but might we sit and talk for a few moments?"

"Can I get you coffee or tea?"

"Thank you, Abraham. Tea would be great."

I returned after a moment, served Lori her tea, and settled in across from her.

She took a sip, peering over the rim. "Abraham, I just want to thank you for the time you spent with Patrick. I have to tell you he's sort of like a different person. I know that sounds weird, but it's true. All he does now is talk about someone named Cindy and what she coached him to do differently and how much more productive he's being at work."

I nodded.

"Now, don't get me wrong," she continued. "I'm not complaining. It seems Cindy is very, very good at what she does, and I'm telling you that Patrick needed something to come along." She sighed. "He was at the end of his rope."

"Well, Lori, I'm quite happy that Cindy has been able to support Patrick. She is wonderful indeed. I'm guessing I'll see Patrick again soon . . . and maybe the boys, too?"

"Patrick said he is coming in this weekend for breakfast. I don't know about Luke or Joey."

"I'll look forward to seeing him, and the boys are welcome anytime." I paused for a moment, taking a sip of my coffee. I looked up at her. "And how are *you*, my dear?" Our eyes connected and hers filled up.

She took a deep breath, shaking her head. "I'm okay. Just okay." She took a deep breath. "Patrick doesn't know I'm here.

I'm not even sure why I'm here. I just felt a need to talk to someone. I . . . I know we're strangers, but Patrick said there was something special about you. So, here I am. Maybe we can keep this chat a secret . . . for now."

I smiled easily. "Sure. Whatever you want."

She dabbed her eyes with her napkin. "Patrick and I have had a few rough years. He was unhappy at work when we lived out east. Then, since we got here, his only focus seems to be work. He says he's doing it for the family . . . but he doesn't see how much he's investing into his career and how much he's *not* investing into us. We—he and I—were a couple long before his current career, and I tell him I believe we have to be strong with one another . . . our relationship has to be strong so we can work through things together . . . we need to be first to and for one another. If not . . .," she faded off and gazed out the window, then turned back to me.

Johnny approached the booth, looking first at Lori. "Sorry to interrupt, ma'am," he turned to look at me, "but can I talk with you for a minute?"

Lori stood. I put a hand on her wrist. "No, stay, this will take a minute." She sat and I walked away with Johnny. I returned and sat. "So, because of this tension, you're okay, just okay?"

She smiled through her moist eyes. "I'm sorry."

"For what?"

"I don't know." She paused and looked away, then back to me. "I just don't know if I can stay . . . with Patrick. I feel like a single woman even though I'm married, and that's not what I signed up for." She paused again. "I need to get going."

As she stood, I looked at her. "Would it be okay to give you a hug?" I asked.

She wiped her eyes. "Yes, I'd like that."

We hugged for a moment and, as we separated, I offered her this: "Lori, I understand why you came to talk today, and I get it. I don't think I've helped you much today, but be patient a while longer, it will all be okay."

She smiled a bit. "I hope so."

I smiled back. "Maybe let go of hope . . . and just trust." She touched my arm as she walked past me to the door.

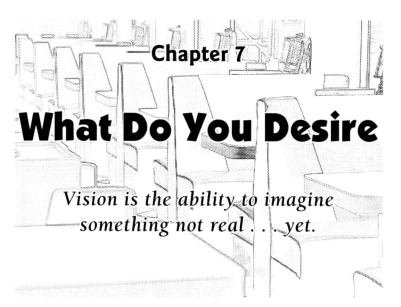

Chapter 7

What Do You Desire

*Vision is the ability to imagine
something not real . . . yet.*

A FEW DAYS later, we were moving around pretty good handling
the breakfast rush when Patrick walked in. He went to the re-
stroom first, then smiled at me when he returned and settled into
a table by the window. Gwen took his order, and just after he
finished eating, I had a lull so went to sit with him.

"This seat taken?" I asked.

"Yes, saving it for you. How are you, Abraham?"

"I'm well. How are you?"

"Pretty good. Work is getting more under control each week.
It sure is amazing how some simple changes in my thinking and
working has really created some focus for me. That time with
Cindy was life changing. I know that sounds cliché. But there's
no question I'm moving faster and easier, as we discussed after
our cooking lesson." He laughed. "That was quite a clever way of
getting me to see what I was *not* doing."

"I do my best."

"I just feel like the actions I'm working on are the right ones and I'm getting them done faster. It feels good. And a few of my team and colleagues have commented that I seem calmer. Even Cole, the CEO at Smith, has mentioned how things are going much better." He paused. "I just noticed the sign you have hanging in the hallway leading to the restrooms. Is that new or did I miss it the other times I've been here?"

"It's been there for a long time. Guess you just weren't ready to read it before," I said. "Yes, a good one—*All that stirs in the unconscious desires to become real*. I believe it was Jung that offered us that thought to consider. Good message, right?"

He nodded.

"Let me ask you about what the sign suggests," I said. "Patrick, what do you desire?"

He answered quickly, nervously. "You mean what do I want?"

I shook my head. "No. Too many people don't get what they want. At least, that's what I hear in here a lot. I mean what do you desire?" My eyes stayed on his until I saw him look away. I caught Gwen's glance as she was coming our way and gave a slight headshake that she recognized. She diverted toward the kitchen.

"Patrick, I'm glad your work with Cindy is going well and providing value for you, but there is more you might consider. I use the word desire because it is the next level of wanting," I paused, "a deeper level. And a more powerful one."

"Seems kind of self-help-ish, Abraham. No offense."

"None taken. I understand what you say, but I firmly believe that many people operate from the want level. And it's been my experience that these folks are not as fulfilled as others. They also bitch more. For me, wanting is a cup of coffee or a new pair of running shoes. Desire," I paused, "is a strong feeling of wanting to have something, or for something to happen, to occur. I believe it's people like Gandhi, Jobs, Jordan, the Wright brothers, Ruth Fertel, and many others that know the difference between want and desire."

"Okay, I'm kind of getting where you're going." Patrick nodded. "But who is Ruth Fertel?"

I smiled. "Yes, Ruth was the divorced, single mother trying to figure out how to earn more money back in 1965 to send her two teenage sons to college. Ignoring the advice of her banker, lawyer, and friends, she mortgaged her home to buy a restaurant in New Orleans."

I smiled, enjoying the silence and Patrick's building curiosity.

"And?" he finally asked.

"And," I continued, "the name of the restaurant was Chris Steak House."

Patrick just shook his head. "I'm guessing later changed to Ruth's Chris Steak House?"

"Wow, you are a bright one." I laughed. "Yes, that's the one; posted revenues of over three hundred million this year. You see, Patrick. It's desire that creates an energy and a focus in people that inspires them to create what they want in spite of any obstacles—I'd bet Ruth Fertel and the others knew this. I don't believe this exists in just wanting something. It's not a strong enough feeling to endure."

"I think I've got it. Abraham, what do you desire?"

I smiled. "Oh, not much; pretty simple for me now. Although this principle has served me well over the years. Patrick, I desire to help and support people. I desire to lead with love."

Patrick's gaze suggested he was thinking deeply about this. I glanced at the iPhone resting on the table. Patrick saw me and looked at the phone and then back to me.

"What?" he inquired.

"Oh, nothing. I notice that you're still on your phone a lot. I'm wondering if you even tasted your breakfast."

"Breakfast was good. I'm just trying to stay ahead of some things and catch up on others. Is that wrong?"

"Not sure. If I said that, then I'd be in judgment and that's not something I like. But do me a favor and take a look around at the people in here sitting by themselves. What do you notice about them?"

Patrick began scanning the diner. He saw Cliff on the other side and waved when their eyes met. Emily sat only a few tables away and they smiled when Patrick looked her way. Two others did the same thing. Patrick turned to me. "So, they're by themselves and they look friendly."

"And relaxed?"

He nodded his head. "Yes, I guess they looked relaxed."

"What else do you notice about them?"

He scanned the diner again. "Abraham, you got me again. Where is this going?"

"Their phones."

He looked again and back at me, puzzled. "Their phones, what are you talking about. I don't see any."

I closed my eyes for a few seconds, letting a grin appear across my face.

"Shit," Patrick said shaking his head. "I got it." He paused. "But what's the lesson here? Wouldn't it be better for them—more productive—if they did some work while they're here? Then they'll have less to worry about the rest of the day."

"A valid question. They are doing work . . . so to speak. They are contemplating their vision . . . and enjoying the stillness they've created. Some may even enjoy their food!"

Patrick shook his head. "The stillness part I get. But contemplating their vision? Whaddya mean? The only people I hear talk about visions are senior execs. Or crazy people."

"No, I don't mean a company vision or mental instability. I mean *their* vision. I know each of these wonderful people and have spent time with them as I am with you. Before they came here for breakfast today, they read the vision they'd written for themselves. Now in their stillness, they're thinking about the gap between current reality so their vision becomes more real to them."

"Okay. I'm lost," he said in a frustrated tone. His phone buzzed and he glanced at it. Then back to me. "Damn, you got me again." He turned the phone off and slid it into his back pocket.

"Patrick, may I ask you a question?" I said. He nodded. "Where is all this action and activity and focus you have heading? If I see you six months from now and ask you how life is and you reply, 'wonderful,' and I ask why it's wonderful . . . how would you answer?"

He thought not long and began, "I don't know. I guess—"

"Stop right there!" I interrupted. "Those are the five words almost everyone begins with. It amazes me that people don't *know* what they want to create for themselves . . . for their families . . . for their teams and clients. It's amazing when Cindy explains this concept of a vision in her workshops, then allows people twenty minutes to begin developing theirs. She says you could hear a pin drop, and the 'aha' moments these people have are great."

"Well, I have some corporate goals," he offered.

"Not the same thing. And when was the last time you looked at them?" I challenged.

"I don't know. I guess—" He caught himself, shook his head, and smiled. "Those five words again. I guess a few months ago."

I continued, "And what about Lori and the kids, and your health and your travel and relationships?" I paused. "And your surfing. When is that going to happen?"

Patrick was again shaking his head. "I think I got it. I have no idea—or not a clear one—of what I want for myself and my family. So how can I trust that what I'm working on is what I should be working on?"

"What do you *wish* for your family? Or desire?"

"Desire," he answered.

"Desire, indeed, that's it. So, one more question and then I must get back to work." He nodded. "How about we go surfing tomorrow morning? I can get this place covered. I'll meet you in the parking lot at El Porto bright and early at 7:00. Good?"

"Um, I don't know. I guess—" He stopped. Then, started again. Very firmly he said, "I guess I trust you enough to know I will get something good out of this. And if nothing else, it will get me out in the water. So how can I say no? It's at Manhattan Beach, right?" I nodded, and then he smiled. "I'm sure I'll see you tomorrow morning then!"

* * *

The next morning I arrived earlier than Patrick and caught a few waves before he got there. The look on his face was priceless as he sat on the beach next to his board, watching me cruise across a wave all the way to the beach, stopping just a few feet from where he sat. I stood in knee-deep water.

He looked away, then to me. "This is getting crazier. I think I should find a new place to eat breakfast."

"What—and miss out on all this fun? Come on, Patrick, if you had not met me, you'd probably be. . . ." I paused. "Oh, never mind. Let's go get some waves." I turned and paddled toward the white waves rolling in.

"Wait," yelled Patrick. "I'd probably be what?"

I turned and yelled back as he paddled toward me, "You'd probably be working right now." I'm not certain, but I think I heard Patrick mumble, "Yep, probably right."

The waves were great that morning—some chest to head high with smooth faces, thanks to an offshore breeze. Patrick surfed well. The joy of the experience lit up his face. I was sitting on my board gazing toward the horizon when he paddled up next to me.

"Thank you."

"For what?"

"For a lot, but right now, thanks for getting me out here. I cannot believe *this* is here most mornings . . . and I'm not. I'm definitely going to get the boys down here."

"What about work, though? And all your e-mails and to-dos?"

Patrick smiled as he spotted a wave and began paddling to it. He turned his board, and just as he was getting to his feet, he looked over and yelled, "It will all be there when I get back."

This made me smile. I caught the next wave in and met Patrick on the beach.

* * *

I pulled my wetsuit down to my waist and sat in the sand. Patrick joined me. "Abraham, that was just great. Thanks again. I'm thinking that you got me out here so I could think more about my vision. Right?"

"This time *you* got *me*," I replied. "And yes, it would be good if you began thinking more about what you desire and started developing a vision for what you want to create over the next six months. What do you want to be real in your life—both at work and in your personal life? I heard you start it already there this morning." I said, pointing to the waves.

"Really? How?"

"Well, you said you were definitely going to get your boys down here."

He looked at me and shook his head. "Keep going."

"It's really quite simple, Patrick. You imagined surfing with your boys and it's not yet happened . . . so, that's part of your vision. Now just fill in the rest of your life."

"The rest of my life? Wouldn't it be good to focus on just one thing at time? I'm organized enough now that I know can make time for getting the boys down here. Shouldn't I work on that one thing first then add other things as I get better?"

"That may sound logical, but it's been my experience that the piece-by-piece approach doesn't work so well in the real world. Say you brought your boys surfing the next few weeks. Then the world and all its 'noise' starts to chip away at your surfing time, and suddenly you realize you haven't surfed in months. Trust me, that is how it works."

"What's the alternative?" he asked.

"Here's what I want you to do." I paused. "You up for more homework?"

He laughed, the lines by his eyes more pronounced in the sunlight. "I was going to say 'I guess so' but realized I'd better say 'sure.' And I'm guessing that 'no' is not an option." He grinned.

I winked. "Not true. No is always an option, but like all choices it just comes with its consequences."

Patrick was looking past me to the ocean so was not able to see the woman standing next to the black Range Rover in the parking lot. I saw her and I knew she saw me. She gave a slight wave, as I did back to her. "Patrick, do you remember the question I asked you about your vision?"

He looked unsure so I let him off the hook. "You know . . . If I see you six months from now and ask you how life is and you reply, 'wonderful,' and I ask why . . . how will you answer?"

"Oh, that one. Sure, sure."

I smiled as the woman got into the Rover and it pulled away slowly.

"What are you smiling at?" Patrick asked.

"Nothing in particular, just smiling. Anyhow, here's your homework. Think about what you want to be real in your life six months from now. And remember when Cindy had you write down all the 'stuff' in your life?"

"How could I forget," he said.

"This is going to work the same way. You'll come up with easy ideas quickly, but then you'll have to push yourself to think more deeply and broadly about everything you desire in your life."

"What do you mean?" Patrick asked.

"You might come up with a goal of, say, progressing in your career. But I want you to be more specific. Do you want a different job or at least be in line for a promotion? Or to keep your current job but have additional responsibilities? Or, whatever it is. Then think about what you will have to have done—the process—in order to make that career advancement a reality six months from now."

"Okay, I think I get the idea."

"Then do the same kind of pushing into other areas—health, spirituality, family, finances, fun, relationships—everything. Heck, you can even mention me and Cindy if you want!" I said. "And don't just think about these things. You have to write down your ideas as if you were answering that question I posed to you—in what ways is your life wonderful six months from now? In fact, imagine you're doing a newspaper article six months from now reporting on events that have already happened. It's very important to have it written in past tense."

"Do a lot of people do this?" he inquired.

"Nope. I'm pretty comfortable at saying about two percent of folks."

"I wonder why so few?"

"Well, why have you never done this kind of thing before? That answer is the one to your question."

He pondered a moment. "I guess I just never thought about it. And not thinking about it meant I never found the time—correction—made the time to focus on it." I nodded. "One thing I'm learning by working with you and Cindy is that I have to be more intentional about what I want to have in my life. So many times I've failed to do something in my career or life and I used the lame excuse, 'I couldn't find the time.'"

"Very good to hear, Patrick. I told you before that time is never really lost so there's no point in looking for it. What we all need to do is manage our focus . . . what we choose to concentrate on. We can choose to focus on anything at any time; there are just consequences to this choice. We need to be sure the consequences are driving our vision."

"Hmmm. Makes sense. Never really thought about it like this." He stood up. "Knowing you, I expect this vision writing task to be harder than it sounds. When is my homework due?"

"This time next week."

What came next surprised me. Patrick leaned in, a hand on my shoulder, and brought his face close to mine. Two grown men, wetsuits down to the waist. He looked at me and said, "Thanks."

"For what?"

"I think you already know." He stood. "See you next week with my homework."

Chapter 8

It is a PROCESS

*Most people never run far enough on their
first wind to find out they've got a second.
Give your dreams all you've got and you'll be
amazed at the energy that comes out of you.*

—WILLIAM JAMES

THE FOLLOWING MORNING, I was in the diner sipping a cup of tea when Emily stopped in to chat for a bit.

"Good morning, Abraham." She smiled as I stood and gave her a hug.

She somehow managed to look both casual and professional, but I think it was her demeanor that had improved her appearance over the last few months. Still, I opted for a more pointed compliment. "Hello, my dear Emily, you look wonderful. Your hair is just perfect."

"Just takes time and money." She winked. "My stylist is an angel." She must have seen me wince when I sat back down. "What's the matter? You hurt or something?"

"Oh, nothing big. I went surfing yesterday with a friend and tweaked my shoulder. He's actually the guy I told you about."

"How's he doing?" she asked as Gwen came by with her cup of coffee. "Thanks, Gwen." Gwen smiled, leaned down, and whispered something in Emily's ear, giving her a kiss on the cheek as she pulled away. Emily said, "Thank you, Gwen." Her eyes seemed to fill with tears. Turning back to me, she said, "Gwen is fantastic. I know you know that, but she is. So, how is this guy doing?"

"He's actually doing well. Cindy did some great work with him around managing all his stuff. He seems to be getting the shift in thinking he so needed, and the behaviors that come with it."

She looked up after a sip of coffee. "Oh, Abraham, you know I've said it many times, but having a chance to develop a better approach to my own life when you hooked me up with Cindy was life changing. I know a lot of my eating and drinking was to escape from all the chaos I had going on . . . both with my inbox at work and all my other stuff, and the relationship with Seth."

I paused a bit to acknowledge her. "Will you talk with Patrick? I gave him his homework yesterday."

A smile grew slowly as she nodded. "The vision?"

"Yes, the vision."

"That was hard for me." Her face grew serious. "It was difficult to write to myself about what I desired in my life, especially when it came to Seth. And my weight. It just brought up some pain. But once I got rolling, it went well."

"I seem to recall that you found writing in the past tense very powerful," I said.

"You're right about that! It made me stop focusing so much on dealing with my shit and instead created a focus for what I want my life to be like on the other side, so to speak. I still read it at least three times a week." She looked at her watch. "Okay, I've got to roll. Let me know when you need me to talk with—what's his name?"

"Patrick."

"Yes, Patrick. Let me know." She leaned down and kissed my cheek. "Love ya, old fella."

"Thanks, love ya back." I smiled; I liked when she called me that.

* * *

A week went by and I thought I might see Lori, but she didn't show up. I thought about what might happen with her and Patrick—and while I usually have strong intuition, this time I didn't have a feeling either way.

As he'd promised, Patrick came in to discuss his homework. He walked into the diner wearing shorts, a t-shirt, and flip-flops. His hair was a bit longer than when we first met, and he'd not shaved in a day or two. He approached me, leather folder under his arm, and gave me a brief hug.

We settled into a booth in the corner and I began, "So, you look great, relaxed . . . and disheveled, I might add." He turned his head sideways. "In a good way," I added. We both laughed. "How was your homework? Fill me in."

Patrick took a deep breath and began, "Man, it was tough getting started. I had a hard time remembering to write in past tense, and I was never sure I had everything in it that I should. I must have begun about eight times. But once I got into the writing, it seemed to flow. Do you want to see it?"

"Yes, but not right now. Keep talking about the process you went through."

"Okay. . . . I've never really done anything like this before. I mean, I'm used to setting goals at work. They usually have to fit into some performance metric system—which is a pain in the ass—and they're in bullet point form, with sub-goals, and sometimes even sub-goals for the sub-goals. So it's very hierarchical."

"Not very useful to you then on a daily basis?" I asked.

"Nope. As we talked about before, I rarely review them. But the way you have me incorporate goals into my vision, in past tense, as if they already happened, that was real good. The detail I added was good too; it allowed me to paint a picture in my head about what it would take to accomplish these goals so they really would come true, and get a sense of the fulfillment I'd have once I've achieved them."

"Good. That's exactly what our vision is . . . the painted picture in our mind's eye."

He opened his folder. "Want to hear my vision?"

Just at this moment Emily came up to the table.

"Good morning," she said to us both. I stood and hugged her. "Good morning, Emily, thanks for coming. I want you to meet a friend of mine. Patrick, this is Emily." They exchanged hand-shakes and hellos. Emily slid in next to me.

"Patrick, I don't think I've told you about Emily; she's a wonderful friend I met a few years ago. She's gone through all the same things that you're doing now. I'd like her to hear your vision and I asked her to bring hers as well. You okay with that?"

He sat for moment, taking a deep breath. "Yeah, I guess." He turned to Emily. "No offense, Emily. I just have some personal stuff in here. It might be weird reading it to a stranger."

Emily smiled. "Patrick, I get it. I felt the same way a few years ago when I had to read mine in a similar situation to this. But I recall that even though it was uncomfortable for me, there was an energy created for me by 'putting it out there' so to speak. It was as if I read my vision for the world. That may sound weird, but that was the case." She paused. "And I'll offer this . . . how about if I read the vision I'm working on to you first? Then I can stick around to hear your vision or I can leave, whichever you choose."

"You don't need to share your own vision with me," he said.

"But I want to. It's not like I go around walking up to strangers on the street and say, 'Excuse me, but may I read my vision to you.'" We all laughed. "It's just that the more people I let know what I'm up to creating in my life, the more focus and accountability I generate for myself. So you'd actually be doing me a favor."

Emily read her vision and there were two parts that Patrick said resonated with him. Here they are:

Professionally, it was my best year. I moved fast and easy with regards to my work and managing my projects and actions. The thinking and resulting behavior from my work with Cindy has now become unconscious, it's second nature . . . I just do it. I led my team to our best year in revenue—we were the top in the country—and my income exceeded $350,000. I supported Ariel in her career and she was promoted to DM. Our celebration was wonderful and I was humbled when she said, "I couldn't have done it without you." The launch of Zigmatec went extremely well. John told me, "Em, you should be very proud of yourself and your team. This was the finest product launch I've seen." With this extra income and the money I saved the past two years, I was able to purchase that rental property I've been looking at. My tenants are great, and the monthly payment actually exceeds my mortgage by $200. I'm excited for next year and have my eye on another promotion for myself.

Seth and I are divorced, it's final. And I sit here today very, very okay with it. There were times when I was a mess throughout the year, but I was very aware in those times; I got back to my vision and what I desire. Seth was and still is on his journey. I will always love and support him. I have moved on and made peace inside myself with it. There is no traction in the past, right? Right! I've continued to focus on my career and health and not on another relationship right now. I'll be ready when I'm ready.

After she finished her last sentence there was silence. A wise coach I know up in Santa Barbara always says, *Let silence do the heavy lifting.* We did, Emily and me. She knew it too. After a long pause, Patrick spoke.

"Wow. Thanks, Emily. That was powerful. Mine's not that good. I don't think I was as honest with myself as you were in your statement—"

Emily interrupted him. "Patrick, 'good' is a judgment," she said. "Let that go. You've written your draft, right?" He nodded. "So give yourself a break. This took me about four or five edits, plus I've been doing it a few years. Yours is just right the way it is. Would you like to read it?"

"Sure." Patrick read his vision and we discussed it afterward. It was lacking in the vivid detail that Emily had, and Patrick realized this. We also challenged him on the relationships he desired to have with his two sons and his wife, Lori. There wasn't much mentioned about them in the draft. He made some edits as we talked, and we could see his vision was growing stronger and clearer, and that he became more excited about the process.

Eventually, Emily said she had to leave and stood up from the table. We all agreed to meet a week later to hear and discuss Patrick's edits.

As we exchanged hugs, Patrick asked, "Em, can I ask you one last question before you go?"

"No problem." She smiled.

"In your vision, you describe your divorce. Forgive me for asking, but don't you see that as a failure?"

"No forgiveness needed, Patrick. Good question." Her tone grew serious. "What I've learned in this process is that turning a vision into reality is not all rainbows and unicorns. There are situations in your life that you decide need to change because it's the right thing to do for you. And, believe me, I worked at it; wish Seth would have a bit more, but he didn't see anything wrong. The way I see it, my vision of divorcing Seth does not represent a failure. Just the opposite, in fact. Staying in a relationship that isn't working, where both people aren't committed to it, would be the failure." She paused, looking away and then back to Patrick. "I'm still on this journey, Patrick, figuring it out as I go. I imagine you're doing the same."

As she turned to leave, Patrick wore a thoughtful expression. "Thank you."

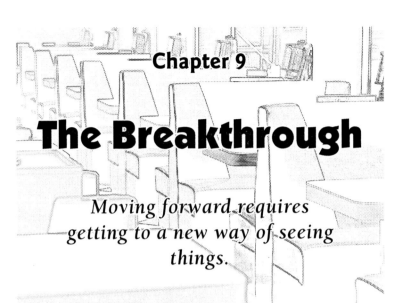

Chapter 9

The Breakthrough

Moving forward requires getting to a new way of seeing things.

THE WEEK WENT quickly as I had much business to attend to both at the diner and with my other interests. I did get in two more surf sessions and they were fun and so good for my Soul. I wish people would tend a bit more to their Souls.

Patrick arrived as scheduled after the breakfast rush had finished. Emily and I were already seated in a booth.

"Good morning, Abraham. Good morning, Emily. How are you two?"

"I'm fine, Patrick. You're looking well. Very relaxed, even peaceful."

"That's because I don't have to do any work today and I'm taking the boys surfing when we're done here."

"That's great," I said. "We'd better not waste time then, since the waves aren't waiting. You ready to talk about your vision?"

Patrick reached into his bag and pulled out his leather folder, placing it on the table. "I've got to tell you, Abraham, this vision writing exercise is the best thing I've ever done in my professional career . . . in fact, probably ever! I feel so focused on what it is I want to accomplish by the end of this year. Getting into the details that you and Emily coached me about last week made a huge difference. I can't get the words to explain it, but it just does something for me . . . to me."

"Yes, it does, I feel the same way," agreed Emily. "I'm looking forward to hearing what you've written for yourself and your family. Would you like to read it to us?"

"Absolutely." Patrick pulled out his reading glasses, took a deep breath, straightened in his chair, and began.

December 31, 2016

Dear Patrick,

Wow, what a wonderful 6 months. Ever since I walked into Abraham's Diner that rainy morning back in March things have been different . . . for the better. I know now why I finally went there for breakfast after I'd heard about it for almost a year from other people . . . I was supposed to meet Abraham.

Since getting out of school, I was so focused on my career and making money . . . now I realized I was not investing in myself, in my own development. I don't mean as a professional, but as a person. I did that this year, and I'll do it now until I die. I considered each area of my life and how I want it to be.

I've read quite a few books now that I've been meaning to read, Man's Search for Meaning *was at the top of that list. I also enjoyed* Back from Heaven's Front Porch. *My TV watching is down dramatically, as I realized I used to do it just to numb out and escape all the work I still had to do that was a tangled mess up in my head and my inbox.*

Work is good; it remains a fast-paced environment with tremendous volume. My work with Cindy has paid off tremendously. I'm certain I've saved 6 to 8 hours a week by adopting some new thoughts about "how" to work. My control and focus on the work I need to get done is at an all-time high . . . and it feels great. The contract renewal with Smith, Inc. was in jeopardy this year and I'm certain my new way of working and thinking generated a focus and calm that allowed me to lead our team through this challenge and re-sign Smith. I've been the driver in getting Cindy into our firm to run workshops for others, and my boss told me, "Now, that's a great example of leadership. We need more partners to work on their development and the development of their people, while also moving the business forward." He's alluded to my next promotion taking place in the coming year. Our team of people exceeded their business goals—while working less and increasing their fulfillment with life outside of work. I'm proud of them all and let them know this consistently. I was able to influence enough of the right people to have

Mary promoted this past fall . . . it was great. She did the work; I just supported her in her vision. Each person on my team has written their vision, and I believe it was the best 'team-building' exercise ever when we each shared ours with the others.

Joey and Luke and I are surfing at least once a week . . . often more. It's great to have this time to get to the beach and just talk. Sometimes our conversations are light-hearted, while other times we talk about the struggles of their lives. This is one of the best things that has come out of my work with Abraham. Being a dad is the most important "job" I have, and I'm thankful I've realized this. It's midway through the b-ball season and Joey's doing great on the team. I'm happy to support him in that and get to nearly every game. Luke's interest in writing has increased and he lets me read his short stories. He has some great ideas and his writing is easy to read, and really makes me feel like I'm "in" the story. We're going to tour a few colleges next year with both of them just to get the process started . . . it will be fun.

I've continued to serve on the parish council at church and support them with their financial plan. We're actually ahead of goal to raise $600,000 for our capital campaign. As a family we also volunteered to serve meals to the homeless in LA over the Thanksgiving weekend. I could tell the boys were moved and reflective after the experience.

My health is really good. For years I watched my weight go up, but these last six months it has gone down . . . 11 pounds to be exact . . . and it's staying off this time. In addition to the surfing, I'm also running two to three times a week. I reduced my carbs and am just more focused on eating more fruits and salads . . . and I have to say it's good. I enjoy this new way of eating and not feeling stuffed. I ran the OC 10-miler in October, and will make it an annual.

I really found value in embracing the stillness that Abraham talked about when I asked what Gwen was doing. I took my first retreat to a great place in Montecito called The Immaculate Heart Center for Spiritual Renewal. I stayed two nights in the Porch room and turned off all my electronics . . . it was wonderful. I'll do it again every year. It was renewing for sure.

I've begun meeting with Joe, our financial guy, every quarter and we've made some nice changes to our investment strategy. I'll buy some investment real estate in Q1 next year. We began looking around in November.

At this point, Patrick paused and looked up. His eyes filled.

"You okay?" I asked.

He took a deep breath, said, "Yes," and continued.

As for my relationship with Lori, it's as close to the way it was when we met. Much better than it has been for a long time. I realized my focus was on many things other than Lori. She was not a priority for me, and now I've made her that . . . as she should be. It was not that I didn't love her; I just took her for granted. We've spent much more time together, just talking. We rode bikes to Abraham's diner almost every weekend for breakfast, and sat on the porch many evenings for a bit. We even got her a wet suit and board and she took some surfing lessons. It was great the first morning she came out with the boys and me. It kept me smiling for days. Our relationship requires work and focus . . . and while she knew this all along, I'm so glad I came to know it too.

So these past six months have been wonderful. Abraham offered some simple wisdom on managing myself and my stuff to get me more control, focus, and inspiration . . . and I'm thankful. Life is no longer as "hard" as I made it. It's a gift, and I enjoy every day!

Be well

Patrick

There was silence. Patrick stood with his coffee mug and walked to the service station and filled it. He slid back into the booth. "So, what do you think? Did I get it right?"

Emily piped up first. "Patrick! We talked about the whole judgment thing last time. If all you just read to me will make you happy and fulfilled as it becomes your reality . . .," she paused, "then you got it right."

"Oh, it does, and it will. When I read this I am inspired. I feel more confident and resilient in working through difficult issues. It provides me focus and a perspective that I don't believe I ever had. Thanks to you."

"I'm with Emily," I said. "It's obvious that your vision was well thought out and you've developed one that is realistic . . . and inspiring. You'll likely add more detail as you continue to understand and use the value of developing your vision. It's a process. Well done, Patrick."

While he was speaking, Emily had reached into her bag and pulled out a stethoscope that she hung around her neck. She grinned slightly as she looked at Abraham, who grinned as well.

"There's one more piece of your education that you may want to consider," she said. "Want to hear about it?"

Patrick looked at Emily, then to the stethoscope hanging from her neck, then to me, then back to Emily. He smiled and shook his head. "I guess. This should be interesting."

Emily stood and took a step to stand next to Patrick on the other side of the booth. She placed the stethoscope in her ears, then the end of it against the side of Patrick's head; she closed her eyes. Patrick looked at me; I just nodded, still grinning. Emily began to make some noises and say a few words. It sounded like this: *Hmmmm. Oh, okay. Wow. Really, okay, we may have to work on this.*

After a few minutes she opened her eyes, removed the stethoscope from her ears, and took her seat next to me in the booth. She took a deep breath, and then looked at Patrick.

"Patrick, my dear, your vision is really strong, and I know that Cindy has supported you in getting some new thinking and behaviors in place relative to managing your stuff." Patrick nodded. "But we also must consider how we manage ourselves. It's what Socrates offered us many, many years ago when he said 'know thyself.'"

"Okay, Em, thanks," said Patrick. "But what the heck is this stethoscope all about?"

"It's quite simple. We're having some fun with you as I put the stethoscope to your head and made some observations . . . as if I could hear what was going on in your head . . . in your thoughts. So, Patrick, if Abraham and I could indeed hear your inner voice, what would we hear? What are your beliefs about your vision and the process of turning it into a reality?"

"I don't know, I guess. . . ." Patrick caught himself as I laughed. "Those five words again, right? I believe my vision is a good one and I can make it real. I'm just a bit mad that it took me this long to get clear on my priorities about work and my family."

"Okay, and what else? What about your work with Cindy? And your role at work and the demands and travel?"

Patrick took a deep breath, then looked back to Em. "Cindy's work is good and I'm doing okay with it, I just hope I can keep it up. And I guess the demands of work will be the same, and probably more, when my promotion comes, so I'll have to stay focused on not getting back to my old work habits."

"Okay, good. Here's the thing. . . ." Emily paused and turned to Abraham. "How about you offer it to him?"

"Sure. Patrick, the last thing that Em and I want to talk with you about as you work on your vision is this: our visions guide us, for sure, and our lives are enriched as we turn them to reality. Here's the thing. Our reality and outcomes are a result of the actions we take. What you do every day is what determines the reality of your life. And the actions we take come from how we feel, what emotions we're experiencing."

Patrick nodded. "Got it, makes sense. But where do our emotions and feelings come from?"

"Ah, yes. Great question. Our emotions come very simply from the beliefs we hold about our lives, our circumstance, and the world as it relates to us. And these beliefs form our mindset . . . or what's often called our fixed mental attitude. And it's this attitude, or disposition, that predetermines our responses to and interpretations of situations."

"So you see, Patrick," Em jumped in, "your beliefs must not limit you, or create unhealthy mindsets for you. They're the starting point for the reality we create in our lives. You can have the most wonderful vision developed, but your energy and the actions you take won't support turning it to reality. So don't hold the belief that your work with Cindy won't stick, or that you won't be able to handle the greater responsibility that comes with your promotion. Believe what will support it."

Patrick was silent for a moment. "I think I get it. Like positive thinking, right?"

"Well, that's not the way I see it," Em said as she leaned in toward Patrick. "Positive thinking to me is just that . . . thinking. By developing yourself a bold, clear vision, and then working to eliminate beliefs that don't serve you . . . you create a positive focus for yourself. You see?"

Patrick took a deep breath. "Yes. I'm getting it. Holding a positive thought or thoughts is really important, but we need our beliefs and mindsets strong . . . and of course we need to take action."

Emily and I looked at one another and replied in unison, "You got it."

I wrapped up our conversation in this topic. "Patrick, it may seem to you that we just dropped this mindset and belief theory on you, and we did. I'm certain we'll work on it more in the future as the opportunity presents itself."

"And it will," Emily said. "And this is a good thing."

"Think about some of the folks I mentioned when we discussed want versus desire. Research suggests that over sixty to seventy percent of new restaurants fail in the first few years. I'd be willing to bet Ruth didn't hold that belief when she bought her first steak house. And I know Steve Jobs held strong beliefs about his team and their innovation and technology when he returned to Apple and challenged them to create a device smaller than a deck of cards that holds ten thousand songs."

Patrick smiled. "Love the examples, Abraham, the iPod sure got Apple rolling again. I see what you're saying. I'll be sure to be more conscious of the beliefs I'm holding."

"Okay, I've got to get going. Gonna hit a yoga class this morning." She turned to Patrick. "It's really been a pleasure getting to know you, Patrick. My sense is you are going to have a really great next year, with many more to follow."

Patrick and I stood to hug Emily. Patrick stood back after his hug, his hands still on her shoulders. "You are one special lady, Em, we'll talk soon. Love ya. And thank you."

Emily smiled through her surprised look. "Wow, cool. Love you too, Patrick, but all I did was offer some things . . . you considered it, and did the work."

She turned, giving me a quick hug. "See you, old man, and you know I love you."

As Emily waved to us through the window, Patrick asked, "Abraham, I know we're done here for today, but would you be willing to share your vision with me?"

I smiled and pulled two multi-page, folded documents from between the menus in the wire holder on the table.

Patrick just shook his head. "Really?"

I chuckled. "Just had a hunch you may want to hear it. But if it's okay with you, I'd like to read you both the first vision I ever wrote and my most recent one. Sound okay?"

Patrick nodded.

I carefully unfolded the brownish, dry paper and was ready to begin as Patrick interrupted.

"Well, I'm guessing this is the first vision you wrote. That or it's the Dead Sea Scrolls." We both laughed.

"Yes, this has been around for a long time." I began to read slowly. *"December 31st, 1975. Dear Abraham. This past year was one of the best I've had since moving to California. I owe much of my accomplishment this year to my friend, Sam Jennings. Writing this vision letter is actually something I did because of Sam's mentorship. . . ."*

I glanced up after the first page and noticed Patrick's looks of awe and surprise. I read the other two pages. When I finished, he sat in silence with his mouth open. I grinned slightly and tilted my head to encourage him to share his thoughts.

He did. "Wow, just wow. You wrote your first vision back in 1975?" I nodded. "And you've done one every year for the past four decades?"

"Yes. It's been the single most powerful thing I've done in my life."

"And it was the Sam you bought the diner from who taught you about writing down your vision? He must have been something else."

"Oh, Sam was one of the best indeed; always committed to supporting people in what they desired to create for themselves and their family. Don't know if you've ever seen it, but there's a great statue of him in Jennings Park a few blocks from here."

"Yes, I know the place, been there a few times. But never made the connection with the Jennings name and I've never seen Sam's statue. I'll stop and say hi to old Sam next time I run through the park." Patrick paused. "It's just so cool knowing you as I do and hearing how all this started. I'm assuming everything you wrote about in that first vision came true? That you bought the diner

74

from Sam, contributed fifty percent toward the sponsorship of a young student who could not attend college without your help, opened your first investment account, and finished the year with over three thousand dollars in it?"

"Well, I didn't make my investment target that first time around, but everything else came true. It was a long time ago, but I remember it well. It's amazing how much focus and momentum it created as I got clear on the life I was creating here in Southern California."

Patrick shook his head. "Oh, I can only imagine. I'm looking forward to hearing your most recent vision . . . but I kind of want to hear all the other ones before that. I'm guessing you still have them?"

I smiled, letting out a deep breath. "Yes, I do; although, that would take a long time, how about if I summarize those?" Patrick said that would be great, so over the next few minutes I told about all the visions I had developed around bringing my mother and father to California, marrying my dear Susan, and then dealing with losing her after only two years together. I told him about my continued commitment to the community, to my friends and family, to the kids I wanted to support getting into and graduating from colleges and universities, my surfing, my wonderful retreats over the years that have strengthened my Faith, my interest in real estate, and many other areas of my life.

Patrick just shook his head. "Thanks, I feel so thankful for your sharing all of this with me; it makes so much sense. I'm really sorry about Susan."

"Thank you, Patrick. I'll tell you about her sometime if you'd like."

"I would." He paused. "Will you read your most recent vision?"

"Certainly." I folded the brownish pages, placing them to the side, and opened the bright white ones. Again, I read slowly. If Patrick was in shock after the first vision, he was way beyond that now. I chuckled at his look.

"What?" he asked.

"Your look is priceless."

We sat in silence until he spoke, shaking his head. "Oh my God, I can't believe it. . . ." He paused. "I mean, I can. Wow. You're funding the new children's cancer outpatient center down by the beach, and named it in honor of your parents. You give away over a half-million dollars per year to organizations that benefit veterans, the senior citizens, and the homeless. You now sponsor two students every year that would otherwise not be able to go to college, and over the years have sponsored a total of forty-eight. Your real estate holdings—with this diner, parking lot, and your apartment complexes total over thirty-four million dollars in value. Your portfolio should total well over four million dollars by the middle of next year." He shook his head and let out a deep breath. "Abraham, you sure are one wealthy man."

"I sure am. But I don't see my wealth in the dollars, rather I see it as what I've been blessed to do with them," I said. "You see, Patrick, I get that we all need to make money and hit our goals, and pay our bills, and prepare for retirement. This is important; what's more important is how we are—how we live—as we do this, and what we do to support others along the way. We're here . . .," I paused and looked out the window, ". . . for such a brief time. We have to lead with love."

Patrick took a deep breath. "You know, I want to change the last thing I said about you being a wealthy man." I raised my brow. "You are a very special man."

"Thank you, Patrick." I smiled slightly as we rose from the booth. "And do me a favor and let's keep this between us, shall we?"

Patrick nodded. "I promise I will. Just forgive me for being so surprised at what you've created in your life."

"Oh, never be surprised. It's simple . . . we get what we focus on," I said with a wink.

Patrick stood and hugged me. As we parted, I noticed the tear in his eye. He walked out of the diner to the waiting black Range Rover, Luke and Joey smiling from the backseat and waving to me, surf boards strapped to the roof. Lori smiled and blew me a kiss as Patrick jumped into the car and it pulled away toward the beach.

About the Author

DANNY BADER IS an author and speaker who believes it's our approach to life and our principles that allow us to create happy and fulfilling lives.

Danny brings his exceptional interpersonal skills and enthusiasm to help people really understand themselves and create a powerful **vision** to turn into reality. His passion and energy for this is rooted in his own journey of development.

Born and raised in a big loving family outside of Philadelphia, he had an easy life until a tragic accident left his friend dead, and Danny having spent some time in "another place" that he believes was Heaven. Since then, Danny has distilled his philosophy of living a happy and fulfilling life into five principles that he calls *jckrbbt*. Danny uses the five principles of *jckrbbt* as the basis of his thought-provoking, humorous, and inspirational talk, *Creating a Happy & Fulfilling Life,* and an interactive workshop benefiting many people in organizations, *Managing Yourself and Your Stuff.*

Danny is the author of two books: *Back from Heaven's Front Porch: Creating a happy & fulfilling life*, and *Abraham's Diner: Simple wisdom for more control, focus, and inspiration.*

He lives with his wife, three children and dog in Pennsylvania.

To contact Danny about coming to your organization, please email him at danny@dannybader.com

For further information on Danny and his message:

www.dannybader.com

https://www.youtube.com/user/dannybader11